50

COMMON INSECTS

OF THE SOUTHWEST

50
COMMON INSECTS
OF THE SOUTHWEST

Carl Olson

WESTERN NATIONAL PARKS ASSOCIATION
TUCSON, ARIZONA

Library of Congress Cataloging-in-Publication Data

Olson, Carl A.
    50 common insects of the Southwest / Carl Olson.
       p.   cm.
    Includes bibliographical references (p.) and index.
    ISBN 1–58369–042–5
    1. Insects—Southwest, New.   I. Title: Fifty common insects of the Southwest.
    II. Title.
QL475.S68O48 2003
595.7'09791 — dc22

                                        2003061080

The net proceeds from WNPA publications support educational
and research programs in the national parks. Receive a free Western
National Parks Association catalog, featuring hundreds of publications. Email: info@wnpa.org or visit www.wnpa.org

Editorial: Derek Gallagher
Design: Campana Design
Cover Photograph: Rick and Nora Bowers; milkweed bug, *Oncopeltus
fasciatus,* of the family Lygaeidae, which feeds on the seeds of
milkweed. *Oncopeltus* is widely distributed in the United States.
Since it feeds on milkweed, it surely sequesters some of the noxious
chemicals from the plant and advertises its bad taste with the bright
orange and black coloration.
Illustrations: Karolyn Darrow
Printing: Sung In Printing, Ltd.
Printed in Korea

NOTE: Insects are wild animals that are extremely important to the
continued health of an ecosystem. Observe, learn, and understand
their biological roles, but leave them to their space. They do possess
mandibles or beaks normally used in feeding, but also for self-protec-
tion. Many species have also evolved a plethora of chemicals that they
may spray, inject, or disperse to keep away giant animals, including
humans, who may create threat situations to them. Be careful and
alert, for their behaviors may not always be pleasant or expected.

INTRODUCTION

*I*nsects are the most diverse group of animals on Earth today. Their species constitute probably 70 percent or more of the animal kingdom, with a wealth of new species waiting to be discovered and named. Their populations are too numerous to be counted, and their bio-mass dwarfs that of all other animals.

Too often the public has but a single perception of an insect group, not realizing the array of morphological features, behaviors, and variations on a theme. This unfortunately leads to a dislike of many small animals that really are the key to the success of nature.

In *50 Common Insects of the Southwest* I will try to delight you with many of the wonderful insects that make the Southwest a literal haven—or maybe heaven—for entomologists. I hope I can remove the mistaken fears humans have of insects and bring you the joy and intrigue of the insect world. ∾

Art Evans

THE LIFE CYCLE OF INSECTS

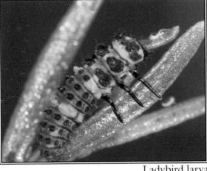

Rick and Nora Bowers

Ladybird larva

Rick and Nora Bowers

Ladybird adults

Insects grow up quite differently than most animals, using a process called *metamorphosis*. Many of the so-called primitive groups—like grasshoppers, mantises, and termites—have a gradual change from egg to nymphal stage. The nymph resembles the adult in most aspects but develops wings externally as the individual grows and sheds its exoskeleton, changing mostly in the enlargement of wing buds.

The dominant groups of insects (more advanced evolutionarily)—including moths, butterflies, beetles, wasps, bees, ants, and flies—show drastic changes in size and form. Their complete metamorphosis starts with an egg, followed by several growth sizes of wormlike juveniles we call caterpillars, grubs, or maggots. This larva then molts into an entirely new stage called a pupa, a non-mobile stage where all larval tissue breaks down and reforms into the adult. To many, these stages may appear as totally different species, because everything from form, food, habitat, and structures is entirely different.

WHERE AND WHEN TO FIND INSECTS

When I lead nature hikes, I don't get far before someone discovers an insect. You have all seen the little creatures and wondered what they are and what they do. But you have only scraped the surface of their habitat. Adults especially must return to their kid days to find insects. Begin by thinking small, getting down to a bug's eye level, or you will miss the world at your feet. Insects live everywhere, but you must learn to look for their different life stages, some unmoving, others cryptic, and some brazenly colored. Take the time to search.

Habitats include any number of things that attract insects. It may be the food and water for survival, or some sort of shelter. Look around and think like a small critter. Would I live under that rock, on that leaf, under the bark of that tree, under this type of soil? Ask yourself *why* an insect might reside in that place. Look there. And don't be discouraged if you don't find them. I have turned many thousands of rocks in my career, thinking "this is going to be a winner," and I have found nothing. Persistence pays off.

You can find insects any time of the year, but once again they may not appear as you thought. Insects are successful because they have adapted their various growth stages to specific time periods. A caterpillar would be doomed if it hatched from the egg when its host plant had no vegetation, as in the winter. Similarly a native bee would not be able to furnish its young with bee bread if it emerged when no flowers were in bloom. Other insects become active when predators may be inactive, or when the temperature and humidity allow for better communication. As I write about the common insects, I will point out some of these activity periods. Once you attune your eyes, you'll begin to notice many more insects. And you'll ask yourself many more questions.

Finally don't be afraid of insects and some of their more formidable relatives, like the scorpions or spiders. Very few insects use people as food (mosquitoes come to mind), and they don't seek you out to simply cause pain. Remember you are the giants and can cause great harm to these small creatures. Learn the kinds that have some defense, like a stinger, sharp mandibles, or a beak. They are few in number and not aggressive.

THE BASIC PARTS OF AN INSECT

HEAD

THORAX

ABDOMEN

LINNAEUS, THE FATHER OF TAXONOMY, NAMED MOST ORDERS OF INSECTS BASED ON FOREWING DEVELOPMENT THUS *LEPIDOPTERA* (BUTTERFLIES AND MOTHS) COMES FROM LEPIDO=SCALE AND PTERA=WING, NICE DESCRIPTORS FOR UNDERSTANDING SCIENTIFIC NAMES.

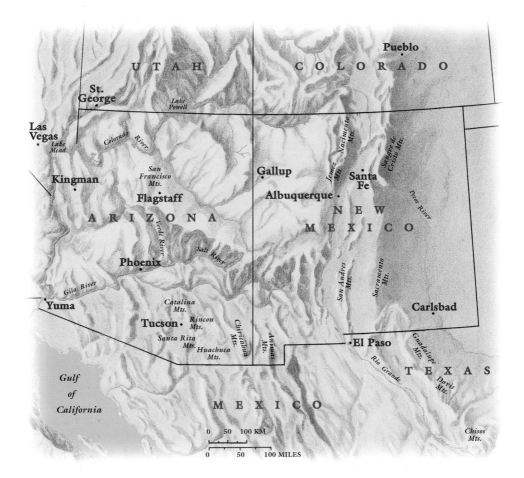

THE VARIED TERRITORY OF SOUTHWESTERN INSECTS

1 · Antlion
Scotoleon niger

Larva

Marty Cordano

Adult

Art Evans

ORDER	Neuroptera
FAMILY	Myrmeleontidae (Myrme = ant, leo = lion)
RANGE	Nevada to Sonora, Mexico, California to New Mexico
SIZE	Male 1³/₄ inches, Female 1 inch

Everyone has probably heard of antlions and may have noticed conical pits found in fine soil or sand in shaded areas. What strange animal is lurking there? It is a creature with sickle-shaped mandibles and an enlarged abdomen that hangs over the thorax, a reverse human belly design. When removed from its pit, this beast moves backwards for escape or to reestablish a pit. At night, it may leave the safety of the pit to actively hunt on the surface, moving forward with the mandibles ready to snap on a prey.

The antlion's pit is its way of trapping unsuspecting ground dwellers, like ants. These fall into the trap, triggering those long mandibles to snap shut on the prey. If it misses its quarry the first time, *Scotoleon niger* will flick grains of sand upward, causing the prey to come tumbling back down into its jaws again. The result is drama underground, as ferocious an attack as a lion ambushing a zebra on the veldt.

And this is only the larval stage. After a long larval life, the Malpighian tubes become silk glands. The larva spins a cocoon, pupates inside this shelter, and transforms into the adult.

The adult antlion is seen by many but recognized by few. It is a nocturnal insect, dull gray, with elongate wings, a very thin body, and short, clubbed antennae. Turn on lights in the summer and these damselfly-like bugs will come, for they, too, are predators, consuming moths or other bugs at the lights.

2 · Bagworm
Oiketicus toumeyi

Charles Hedgcock

Moths and butterflies usually elicit a smile on people's faces because they like the bright colors and the wispy flights of these creatures. The drab and unassuming are easily overlooked, until the caterpillars begin the task of feeding and growing on a favorite plant. So it is with the marvelous bagworm.

Oiketicus toumeyi is familiar to most in its disguised larval home, a silken case decorated with bits of leaf or needles from the host plant. The silk is incredibly tough, protecting the naked black caterpillar while it feeds by popping its head through a doorway to get to the leaves. When the larva is inactive, the case is supported by a silken loop spun over a twig, with the door sewn shut with silk. A small portal below allows fecal material to exit the home.

As the caterpillar grows, it expands its shelter. After a summer of feeding, the caterpillar spins a permanent silken tie to the plant, seals off the anterior opening to form a cocoon, and pupates.

Adult bagworms have a brief lifespan and fly only at night. Only the most avid moth spotters may see one. The flight and mating period is April to June, a rather harsh weather time for most animals of the arid Southwest.

The wingless females remain inside their cases, attracting a male to the bag for mating purposes. They lay hundreds of eggs inside this case, and soon die. The newly hatched larvae exit the bag and soon establish mobile homes of their own.

ORDER	Lepidotera
FAMILY	Psychidae
RANGE	California to Texas
SIZE	Silken case 1/4 to 3 inches

ORDER	Hemiptera
FAMILY	Reduviidae
RANGE	California to Texas
SIZE	3/4 inch

Bee killers are classified as assassin bugs. They are excellent sit-and-wait hunters, capturing a variety of prey, but because they hide in flowers, their encounters are most often with unsuspecting bees or wasps that have come to sip nectar.

Bee killers range from brilliant red and yellow individuals to dull black species. The female seeks plant resins to spread over her abdomen, using them later to cover and protect her eggs. The sticky resins deter predators and parasites. Remnants on the forelegs help in prey capture, acting as a glue to prevent escape. Nothing goes to waste in the insect world.

Reduviids have evolved raptorial forelegs, designed to reach out and grab prey, like praying mantises. These efficient and exceedingly strong legs allow them to capture wasps and bees larger than they are, while a hard exoskeleton makes them virtually impervious to the stings. Next time you stop to smell the flowers, take an extra second to see if this amazing predator has taken up residence there.

Rick and Nora Bowers

4 · Black Witch
Ascalaphus odoratus

Marty Cordano

The moth family Noctuidae contains such members as cutworms, armyworms, underwings, and millers. None will stand out and be remembered except maybe for their numbers. The black witch, though, is unforgettable. This grand moth used to be regarded as a fly-in from Mexico late in the summer, with tattered specimens showing up in U.S. border states. In the last ten years or so, however, researchers have *regularly* found perfect specimens in the United States. It is hard to miss a five-inch-wide, dark-brown moth, marked with lavender bands across fore and hind wings.

The black witch, called *micpapalotl* in Mexico, is an omen of death if it lands on your door. Some of the country people of Mexico harvest the larvae, which they dry, cook, and serve in tortillas with salsa. Such resources cannot be overlooked when protein sources are otherwise scarce.

ORDER	Lepidoptera
FAMILY	Noctuidae
RANGE	Southern United States, Mexico, Caribbean
SIZE	Wingspan 4 to 6 inches

5 · Carpenter Bee
Xylocopa californica arizonensis

ORDER	Hymenoptera
FAMILY	Apidae
RANGE	Southern California to Texas, Nevada, Utah, and Mexico
SIZE	3/4 to 1 inch

Carpenter bees don't work wood, but chew into different types of wood to create nest sites, using anything from soft, rotting tree limbs to agave and sotol flower stalks. *X. californica arizonensis* often uses agave stalks for nesting. The hiker that selects a well-aged agave for a walking stick may be surprised when it starts buzzing.

These large metallic blue-black to black bees are the size of bumble bees, not quite as furry, but equally as blusterous. Come near a nest site and a female will challenge you to a staring match, although she never gets too close.

One seldom sees the males, typically defined with some yellow markings on the face, although the male of one southwestern species is entirely yellow. Males are the first individuals to emerge from the nest in spring, preparing for the mating season by feeding avidly on pollen and nectar.

With the start of nest building in late spring, you'll see carpenter bees grazing the yellow composites and flowering trees that dot the countryside. By this time the males have preformed their duties and have died, leaving nest building and provisioning to the females.

6 · Cholla Long-Horned Beetle
Moneilema gigas

Marty Cordano

Moneilema are flightless beetles, well adapted to life feeding in or on the diverse cactus flora of the Southwest. They possess large pads on their feet that appear almost like snowshoes, giving them a clumsy look but allowing easy movement through the spiny jungle of a cactus. Adults are armor-plated, oblivious to the spiny armament of the cholla and prickly pear. The larvae feed inside the spongy cacti, avoiding spines that would puncture their softer exoskeletons, and eventually pupate at the base of the host cactus.

Moneilema has a smooth black appearance, similar to that of the notorious Pinacate beetles in the Southwest. Some biologists have suggested that they are mimics, gaining some protection as a predator may associate bad odors with the look. A better protection may be their ability to squeak when alarmed or disturbed, a sound produced by rubbing the thorax and abdomen together where ridges have developed. The insect world is indeed full of many sounds.

ORDER	Coleoptera
FAMILY	Cerambycidae
RANGE	Arizona, New Mexico
SIZE	3/4 to 1 1/2 inches

7 · Cicada
Diceroprocta apache

ORDER	Hemiptera
FAMILY	Cicadidae
RANGE	Arizona, New Mexico
SIZE	Body length 1 inch, Wings 1 1/4 inches

Cicadas are more familiar to people for their strident, incessant songs or the strange empty cases left on trees or fences by their nymphs during metamorphosis than for the physical appearance of the adults. Cicadas are with us throughout the summer and early fall because of the staggered emergence of numerous species during this time. To understand that there are many different species, you must listen and discriminate the subtle song variations heard.

Cicadas lay eggs in tree branches, resulting in a slight pruning of the tree when the twig dies. After the eggs hatch, the nymph drops from the tree and burrows into the soil. The juvenile takes 3–5 years (or 13–17 years if they are the well-known periodical cicadas of the East) to develop underground, drinking liquids from roots of plants. Different species will then dig to the surface, usually at dusk or nighttime, find a tree or similar structure to dig their claws into, split open the back of their exoskeleton and magically transform into a winged adult. *Diceroprocta apache* emerges at the end of May.

Males are the songsters. *Diceroprocta* is usually a soloist, sitting in a palo verde tree singing during the hottest times of the day to attract a mate. Other species mass together as a giant choir, creating ear-splitting music both to attract mates and to keep predators from approaching. If an individual is captured by a bird, it emits a shrill scream, and if the cicada is lucky, the bird will open its beak and the cicada flies away. To counteract the heat, cicadas are the only insects known to sweat, having evolved a series of tubes internally to release moisture around them, acting like swamp coolers. They restore water by simply tapping into the xylem of the tree. Only desert species have evolved this adaptation.

Emerging adult

Charles Hedgcock

Kim Wismann

8 · Cochineal Scales
Dactylopius confusus

Kim Wismann

Robert and Linda Mitchell

S cale insects are a mysterious group, to say the least. Widely distributed, problematic, and cursed by many plant enthusiasts, scales are recognized more by their external encasements than by their anatomy. Common names like lac, cottony cushion, or oyster shell allude to their protective shields. Their life history includes a stage termed "crawlers," the time when young move around their host before settling down to a sedentary life of feeding and reproducing.

Opuntia cacti (such as prickly pear) are a common habitat for cochineal scales. Examine the white waxy globs covering a pad and you may see the carmine bag of a bug hidden beneath that white wax, a protection from desiccation in the arid world of cactus. This is a female scale, a feeding machine oblivious to the world. Sometimes under the wax, a predatory caterpillar or a strange ladybird beetle may be found managing this population of scales, both brilliant red from consuming scales. An older scale colony may have rings of silken cocoons around one of the females, signs that winged males will soon be emerging to seek mates.

Cochineal is historically famous for its use by humans. The Aztecs used *D. coccus*, a larger, less waxy species, in their highly developed dyeing industry. When Cortés came to the New World in 1519, this brilliant color caught his eye, and he took it back to Europe. That is why the British army had red coats.

ORDER	Hemiptera
FAMILY	Dactylopiidae
RANGE	Arizona to Texas
SIZE	1/4 inch

9 · Convergent Ladybird Beetle
Hippodamia convergens

ORDER	Coleoptera
FAMILY	Coccinellidae
RANGE	Cosmopolitan
SIZE	3/16 inch

The name "ladybird" originated in Europe more than 600 years ago. In the United States, it became "ladybug." These names have nothing to do with gender, as there are both males and females in all species.

The convergent ladybird beetle is the familiar orange beetle with a varying number of spots on the elytra (hardened forewings). White dashes on the black pronotum (shield behind head) converge toward the back of the shield, thus "convergens."

Ladybirds are the proverbial "good bugs," predators of aphids, scales, and other soft-bodied insects that gardeners get upset with. The larval stage may be the best eating stage, always hungry and searching. The larva has a bead-like texture, and is blue-black and orange in color.

In the Southwest, this beetle is found in huge clusters in the mountaintops, coating trees and rocks in an orange blanket. They stay in the mountains, mostly just sitting, until early spring, when they fly to the valleys below. These adults then mate and seek out emerging annual wildflowers to lay eggs on.

Larva

The populations of aphids that cover these plants supply food for the hatching larvae. March and April are good months to observe this activity, and also to discover the pupal stage of ladybirds. In May, when the desert becomes hot and dry and plants wither, the newly emerged adult ladybirds return to the cool climes of mountaintops, engorge themselves on pollen, then fly to the canyons to spend the rest of the year.

These populations are harvested occasionally, brought down to the valleys, and sold to unsuspecting customers hoping to control aphid outbreaks in their gardens. The ladybirds, when released, are either not hungry or still in a state of diapause (similar to hibernation), and return to the closest mountaintop.

Adult

Charles Hedgcock

10 · Crane Fly
Tipula spp.

Bill Johnson

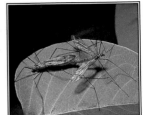

Allan Morgan

Mating pair

ORDER	Diptera
FAMILY	Tipulidae
RANGE	Southwest United States
SIZE	Body length 1/2 to 1 or 2 inches

Giant Alaskan mosquitoes! might be one's guess at first sight of these gangly-legged flies. They have a strange elongated snout and their body appears mosquito-like. As kids we used to call them mosquito hawks, under the misconception that they captured and ate those nasty bloodsuckers. It wasn't until much later I learned that these flies, if they feed at all, are nectar drinkers.

Larvae reside in a variety of habitats, from aquatic niches to soils, feeding on organic matter. The terrestrial larvae are called "leather jackets" due to their roughened exoskeletal texture. If winter rains are plentiful, the underground larvae get plenty of food and huge populations of the crane flies emerge in the spring.

Adults may remind one of daddy longlegs because of their stilt-legged appearance, but also because their legs break off at the slightest resistance, allowing escape from spider webs or other predators.

Tipulidae is the largest family of flies with more than 1,600 species in North America alone. The oddest of this group may be the winter crane flies—wingless, spider-like creatures that emerge when the snow flies. They are at home walking across snowfields when more respectable insects might consider seeking shelter from the weather. They produce glycerol—an antifreeze—in their blood, to keep them active.

11 · Creosote Walkingstick
Diapheromera covilleae

Allan Morgan

Crypsis. Mimicry. The creosote walking stick may be the ultimate disguise artist. Try to find one of these in its natural haunt, the creosote bush. They move with the stealth of a chameleon, swaying from side to side as if the wind is blowing the twigs about, picking the time to slowly, agonizingly move their legs. How they get from one place to another is beyond me.

This species, besides having a stick-like body, has extremely long, delicate antennae for sensing its environs. It is colored with greens and browns to match the creosote bark and leaves that it feeds on. Other walkingstick species in the Southwest are hosted by mesquite, acacia, or the typical perennial shrubs that dot the landscape.

Walkingsticks produce large flask-shaped eggs, with a knob at one end, reminiscent of seeds. With some species, these eggs are picked up by ants because of the seed resemblance and taken into the ant nest, where they develop, protected from outside dangers. Once more nature finds creative ways to ensure survival while sharing the wealth.

ORDER	Phasmida
FAMILY	Heteronemiidae
RANGE	Arizona to Texas
SIZE	3 to 4 inches

12 · Desert Cockroach
Arenivaga erratica

Female

Male

The cockroach, or *cucaracha*, although stereotyped as undesirable in urban settings, has many diverse welcome behaviors and haunts in natural habitats. Very primitive roaches are found in moist, rotting logs, eating and recycling wood much as termites do. Other species inhabit caves or forests, and some live in swamps or other aquatic environments, feeding on organic debris.

Desert roaches blend nicely with their habitat, having a mottled sandy appearance. Males are winged and active at night, and may be seen flying around lights in city or country. Females are secretive, wingless, dark brown, and look like robust sowbugs. They share living space in pack rat or ground squirrel dens, burrowing into the loose soil at the nest entrance. They feed on debris and waste left by the larger inhabitants, cleaning up after them.

ORDER	Blattaria
FAMILY	Polyphagidae
RANGE	Arizona to Texas
SIZE	Male 1/2 to 3/4 inch, Female 1/2 inch

13 · Desert Encruster Termite
Gnathamitermes perplexus

ORDER	Isoptera
FAMILY	Termitidae
RANGE	Southern California to Texas, Baja California
SIZE	Workers 1/8 inch, Winged 3/8 inch

Termites are one of the least-loved insects and certainly the most misunderstood. They are social insects, living in large colonies, headed by a queen and king, protected by a small army of soldiers, and dominated by a worker caste that performs all the work needed for a society to succeed, including being nursemaids, groomers, and food gatherers.

Termites are dead-plant recyclers, keeping the land clear of all the material that we found delightful when it was alive. Because most termites live underground, they are also one of the premier soil builders on Earth, helping aerate and fertilize the soil. *Gnathamitermes perplexus* is well known for covering dead plants, usually in the fall after monsoon rains have given the Southwest a drink. Take a walk and look for strange mud encasements on twigs or cactus skeletons on the ground. If some of the mud flakes off, you may see the white workers scatter for protection from the sun's killing rays.

Another phenomenon of this group of insects is the production of winged adults (alates), a way of moving the species into new landscapes. The alates of the desert encruster are tied to the afternoon rains of July and August. Go out in the mist and start looking for clumsy flying individuals. Seek out the hole in the ground from which they are coming, and watch as workers bring these alates to the surface and literally shove them out of the nest. Then watch as nighthawks capture some, or look for large carmine-colored, velvet mites that emerge to feast on the termites after they shed their wings. Some encrusters find mates upon alighting, drop their wings, and scurry off in tandem seeking easy digging to start a new colony.

Derek Gallagher

Kim Wismann

14 · Dung Beetle
Canthon imitator

Marty Cordano

Humans seldom hold insects in much esteem, but the sacred scarab, a dung beetle, enjoyed the status of a god in ancient Egyptian culture. Ancient Egyptians observed the act of dung-rolling by this beetle, and related this behavior to the movement of the sun. The ancient sun god Khepri was seen as a great scarab rolling the sun across the heavens. A flattened scarab model called the heart scarab was placed on a mummy, a symbol of rebirth just as the sun was reborn each sunrise.

The various species of dung beetles require different qualities of dung to use either as food or to create a ball, roll to a safe haven, and deposit a single egg in the ball. The larva hatches inside the dung ball and consumes this rich resource, growing and eventually pupating inside this encrusted, safe home.

Dung beetle adults have modified forelegs with enlarged tibiae for digging and shaping, and reduced tarsi (feet) to prevent them from getting caught in the dung ball. *Canthon* is rather a plain-Jane in the dung beetle world with no horn development in males, only a smooth robust shape. Other species show amazing sexual dimorphism with the males having enlarged horns.

Africa is a rich source of dung beetles, and many have been imported by governmental agencies and released around the world in hopes to increase recycling of the remains of cattle grazing. Unfortunately these imports have impacted the native dung beetle populations by out-competing them for resources. This may not seem problematic, but exotics may have long-term adverse effects that we haven't foreseen. Dung removal is only one part of fitting species together for a healthy environment, as many other animals may rely on native species in ways not observed by people.

ORDER	Coleoptera
FAMILY	Scarabaeidae
RANGE	Arizona to Texas
SIZE	1/2 to 5/8 inch

The fig beetle, erroneously called a green June beetle, is seen across the Southwest during the monsoons of July to September. Adult beetles are fruit and sap feeders, found clustered at a tree weep or consuming prickly pear fruit. This insect was dubbed the fig beetle because it delights in soft, delicate fruits—like juicy figs.

Its jewel-like green underside, and the funny horn on its head, makes *Cotinus mutabilis* quite a treasure to behold. The horn helps open the tough rind of the fleshy fruit, much like a can opener.

The larval stage is a white grub, related to those C-shaped root-feeding scarabs. You are most likely to see the fig beetle larva in rich organic materials or even compost piles. You can recognize it by its strange behavior of crawling about on its back instead of using its short legs.

Allan Morgan

ORDER	Coleoptera
FAMILY	Scarabaeidae
RANGE	California to Texas
SIZE	3/4 to 7/8 inch

16 · Firefly, Lightningbug
Pleotomus nigripennis

Joe Cicero

Larva

It is a common misconception that there are no fireflies in the Southwest, because we don't have the hordes of flashing males so common to a Midwestern lawn. Truth is, our populations have much smaller, more restricted habitats due to the aridity of the area. Also we have species here that do not possess the lamps we so fondly remember.

Several species common to the Southwest do exhibit the familiar male flash calls to flightless females in the grass. These species, *Bicellonycha wickershamorum* and *Photinus knulli*, are found in many of the southern mountain canyons or riparian areas, but their populations are small. The window of activity is typically late in the monsoon season.

By far the most common sighting is that of the larval stage of *Pleotomus*. People in the summer constantly wonder about the eerie green light they observed moving along a canyon road. When they turn a flashlight on the phenomenon, they are surprised to find an alien-looking, armor-plated worm, pink to gray in color, emitting the strange light behind.

This larva feeds on the snail *Sonorella sonora*. It pupates under rocks or tree bark. Females are unknown but probably are larviform, changing little from their juvenile state. Males have a more typical firefly look with non-working light organs.

ORDER	Coleoptera
FAMILY	Lampyridae
RANGE	Arizona to New Mexico
SIZE	Larva 3/4 inch, Adult 1/2 inch

17 · Giant Mesquite Bug
Thasus neocalifornicus

ORDER	Hemiptera
FAMILY	Coreidae
RANGE	California to Arizona
SIZE	Nymph 1 inch, Adult 1¼ inches

Spectacular bugs are the norm for the Southwest. This leaf-footed bug fits the bill, from colors and body designs to odor.

In April, after the mesquites have leafed and flowered, the overwintering eggs of *Thasus* hatch and strange, spindly-legged nymphs with an odd enlargement on the antennae will scramble about the trees, seeking out juicy leaflets from which to drink sap. Soon these tiny blue bugs with a medial orange band have molted into rich red-and-white nymphs, which cluster in packs to intensify their smell, a sweet pungency that may repel predators or attract human curiosity.

Nymphs molt into adults by mid-June, becoming olive drab individuals, still recognizable by the enlarged antennal segment. Males are easily recognized by the enlarged hind femurs banded with orange. This leg design allows the male to establish a firm grip on the female during mating.

Adults lose the striking aposematic colors because they have gained flight for escape. Still the adults don't range too far from mesquites, feeding on the seed pods or tender petioles. Adults may live until the end of monsoons, laying eggs on or near a potential host tree for next year's offspring.

Nymph — Charles Hedgcock

Adult — Art Evans

18 · Gray Bird Locust
Schistocerca nitens

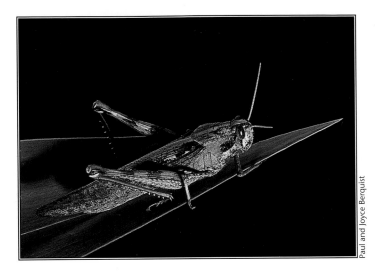

Paul and Joyce Berquist

This species and the green bird locust *S. shoshone* are two of the largest and strongest flying grasshoppers in the Southwest. They are related to the migratory grasshoppers, *S. gregaria*, that are given such negative press when their populations overwhelm the African and Asian continents. The family name, short-horned grasshoppers, describes the antennae, which are not much longer than the head.

These grasshoppers tend to operate in extremely high temperatures, optimal for metabolic efficiency, though their juvenile stages, which are bright green, move to cooler localities as temperatures approach lethal conditions. The adults have special patches (Slifer's patches) of thin cuticle on the abdomen that allow evaporation for cooling.

Schistocerca nitens feed on a variety of plants, from mesquite, creosote, and oak, to short weeds and herbs like ragweed and pigweed, and even crops like alfalfa and cotton. Adults are active from March to November, juveniles usually May to November.

ORDER	Orthoptera
FAMILY	Acrididae
RANGE	California to Texas south to Nicaragua, typical of Lower Sonoran Desert
SIZE	1 1/2 to 3 inches

19 · Greater Angle-Winged Katydid
Microcentrum rhombifolium

ORDER	Orthoptera
FAMILY	Tettigoniidae
RANGE	California to Texas, most of United States
SIZE	2 to 2¹/4 inches

Rick and Nora Bowers

Katydids bring out the child in everyone. Who hasn't been outside on a summer's night and heard the call of the katydid? Loud, insistent, but hidden from view.

Katydids are called long-horned grasshoppers because their antennae, elongate filamentous organs, are longer than their body. The most common ones are green and leaflike, but the variety of colors and shapes that evolve to make this animal more cryptic is never-ending. Jagged patches of browns infringe on the greens, making the katydid appear like a leaf with a chunk eaten off by some other insect. Other genera in the Southwest have very thin wings and extremely long, gangly legs, another tactic to prevent easy detection.

Katydids are songsters, with the males calling to females. They use the forewings, rubbing a scraper device on the right wing over a file on the left wing to create their songs. Ears are located on the front legs at the knee joint. Both genders have these organs, for males may respond to songs too.

Females lay flattened, scale-like eggs on twigs or leaves. The oblong eggs overlap, usually in two straight lines on either side of a twig. This is the survival stage, lasting through winter and hatching when new vegetation bursts forth in the springtime. Katydids feed on a wide variety of plants.

20 · Green Darner
Anax junius

Frederic B. Siskind

Frederic B. Siskind

Insects are fearsome creatures, especially predator insects, but this superficial quality is taken to negative extremes by people. Such is the case for the green darner. Here is a wonderful predator that parents have used to control unruly children, with the threats that this dragonfly will come and sew their mouth shut: thus its popular name Devil's darning needle. Other common names conjure up imaginative associations, such as snake doctor, horse-stinger, *caballitos del Diablo* or mosquito hawk.

This dragonfly is one of our larger species, easily noticed by its green thorax and blue abdomen as it patrols its territory. Typically it cruises about head-high, and if disturbed will shoot into the sky and disappear for an extended period. *Anax junius* requires large aquatic plants like cattails for residence, as females oviposit into the plants, and the juvenile stages escape detection by clinging to the vegetation under the water while waiting for unsuspecting prey to swim past. The juveniles are streamlined and jet-propelled, squirting water from a cavity within the abdomen as they streak after some aquatic insect that has dared to venture too close.

ORDER	Odonata
FAMILY	Aeschnidae
RANGE	California to Texas, most of United States
SIZE	Body 2⅝ inches, Wingspan 4 inches

21 · Green Lacewing
Chrysoperla carnea

ORDER	Neuroptera
FAMILY	Chrysopidae
RANGE	Cosmopolitan
SIZE	1/2 inch

As one walks among the flowers and shrubs, dainty emerald green insects flit upwards to new perches. Closer examination reveals delicate individuals, slender of body with lacy wings and copper-colored eyes.

Females seek out leaves or twigs to lay their eggs on. These mothers are quite ingenious, producing silken strands that hang downward with a single egg attached. Why go to such trouble? The egg hatches into what appears to be a mini-alligator, a larva with sickle-shaped mandibles designed for piercing and drinking juices out of prey. This little eating machine is at the bottom of the silk, and must climb to the leaf. Upon achieving that surface, it begins searching for insect prey, never considering climbing down the next silken stalk, where its brother or sister dangles. Thus each offspring has a chance at survival. The food of these voracious larvae includes aphids, insect eggs, and other insects. Sometimes the larvae are called aphid lions, in reference to their feeding habits.

After much feeding, these larvae seek shelter amidst a curled leaf or other secret space and spin a silken cocoon in which they pupate. Soon more green snowflakes will flitter through the landscape, bringing balance to the ecosystem.

22 · Harvester Ant
Pogonomyrmex barbatus

Paul and Joyce Berquist

Ants are really highly socialized wingless wasps. Common names have simply separated these two forms of Hymenoptera. Ant colonies are all female, except for the special time when winged individuals (alates) are seen swarming after a rainstorm. Those individuals are the royalty, kings and queens, leaving home with a chance of passing on their legacy to a new colony. Males age and die quickly after mating, but the queens may be fortunate enough to find a suitable habitat and begin the next colony.

Pogonomyrmex barbatus clears the ground for about a yard around its single nest opening. This makes the nest easy for you to recognize. By removing the plants, the ants remove the root competition for the nest site. The nest may be more than 20 feet deep, and the side galleries extend outward for many yards. A nest may have upwards of 20,000 individuals, with worker castes dying and being replaced perhaps monthly. Thus one can see how important ants are to the welfare of the soil, aerating and rebuilding enormous areas.

Although harvester ants are seed gatherers and feeders, they also possess a sting (modified ovipositor) and venom that create as intense a pain as any southwestern arthropod. (These are NOT the infamous fire ants that people in the Southeast know all too well.) They are quick to defend the nest site from intruders, roiling out of the single nest opening at the slightest provocation. They sting unsuspecting beetles and others who stumble across the nest site, killing and dismembering them.

A long-established colony will produce a wagon wheel effect, with trails beaten into the ground leading to rich food sources. With six feet on thousands of individuals pounding the soil daily, it is easy to see how they form.

ORDER	Hymenoptera
FAMILY	Formicidae
RANGE	California to Texas, Nevada
SIZE	Workers 3/8 inch, Queens 1/2 inch

23 · Honeybee
Apis mellifera

ORDER	Hymenoptera
FAMILY	Apidae
RANGE	Worldwide
SIZE	1/2 inch

Honeybees are well known, but their cousins the Africanized bees are causing much consternation in the Southwest these days. Historically, European settlers introduced honeybees to America in 1638. The European strain of honeybee was adapted for cool, dry climates and was an excellent honey producer. In South America, a more tropical setting, these honeybees were not as successful. In 1956 a Brazilian geneticist imported a strain of honeybee from Africa to create a new strain for the tropics. It was this strain that escaped and eventually entered the United States.

These "new" honeybees are usually more aggressive and have been tagged by the media as "killer bees," an unfortunate designation. They are very successful pollinators and honey producers, and readily managed today.

Honeybees are social insects, meaning there is division of labor. Workers tolerate males (drones) in the colony for a short time, until new queens are mated, after which they drive them out to die. Worker bees are infertile females who tend cells and new larvae and forage for pollen and nectar. Queens are the reproductive machines. Bees swarm to divide a colony and disperse colonies into new territories. Swarming bees are not aggressive, and bees at work on flowers focus on the task and are seldom disturbed by human presence.

24 · Horse Lubber
Taeniopoda eques

Robert and Linda Mitchell

Robert and Linda Mitchell

The horse lubber is one of the largest grasshoppers in the Southwest. The females, with shortened wings and engorged abdomen, lumber across the landscape, mating, eating and searching for good soil under which to hide their eggs. The males, svelte and mobile, fly from perches when disturbed, creating a vision of flying flowers, the green forewings setting off the brilliant red hindwings.

The eggs hatch in late spring, sending small black-and-yellow nymphs scurrying across the land in search of food. This color pattern sends a message to most predators, "Don't eat me; I taste bad." By August these nymphs are ready to shed one last juvenile set of clothes and make their adult presence known to the world. As adults, they feed on numerous types of plants, extracting toxins that add to their distastefulness.

You may wonder how a day-active black grasshopper survives the desert heat. *Taeniopoda eques* has developed many positions to either increase or reduce the amount of body surface it exposes to the sun. It even uses the warmth of the ground to warm itself in the early morning. When you observe one of these beasts doing strange things with legs or wings, what you see is all part of beating the heat.

ORDER	Orthoptera
FAMILY	Romaleidae
RANGE	California to Texas
SIZE	Male 2 inches, Female 2 1/2 inches

25 · Hover Fly
Volucella isabellina

ORDER	Diptera
FAMILY	Syrphidae
RANGE	California to Colorado, Arizona
SIZE	1/2 inch

Walking through a field of flowers, one cannot help but see the insect activity near many of the blooms. A first glance it looks like honeybees are out doing their job. Closer examination reveals that not all the pollinators are what they seem. Hover flies are the same color as bees, but their bodies are almost translucent, and their flight is much more aerobatic, hovering or darting between the flowers, never really stopping to rest.

Flies are very soft bodied, and thus susceptible to the dangers of predation. Many use mimicry to help them survive, using different wasps and bees as models for this deception.

Larvae of syrphids typically reside in rotting plants. These tough, flattened maggots help the recycling process of decaying vegetation. Others have turned to predation of aphids. My favorite is the rattailed maggot, a group that resides in highly polluted, eutrophic, aquatic haunts. To survive the lack of oxygen, these maggots have an extendible rear end with the spiracles (breathing pores of insects) at the tip. The maggot can extend this tail to the water surface and take in a bubble of oxygen that will last a long time. When the maggots are ready to pupate, they leave the goop and head to drier places, eventually hardening their last larval exoskeleton into a puparium and transforming inside the case.

Rick and Nora Bowers

26 · Iron-Cross Blister Beetle
Tegrodera aloga

Charles Hedgcock

Each spring in April, brightly colored beetles appear in the Sonoran Desert to feed and find proper hosts for their offspring. This is one insect people can't miss because they appear in huge populations and have a brilliant red head and pronotum, contrasting with mottled yellow elytra marked by a strong black cross. This red front looks ant-like and the rear beetle-like. Sometimes as these beetles are running over the hot landscape, they raise their wings and display their black abdomen marked with bright red stripes, making them seem like wasps.

These beetles have a product called cantharidin in their blood, a potential blistering agent, thus the common name. When disturbed, their leg joints ooze blood that to a predator may taste bad or be painful. To a human, it may cause mild blistering. Their bright colors (aposemitism) advertise this defense.

Tegrodera emerges in April from digger bee nests, usually in loose soils. They feed on spring annuals like *Eriastrum*, starting about eleven in the morning and continuing until about five in the afternoon.

After mating, females seek palo verde trees in bud stage, lay eggs at the base of the buds, and then die. The eggs and buds develop together, eggs hatching when the flower opens. Larvae wait in flowers for native bees to arrive, hitch a ride back to the nest, where they stay, feeding on the juvenile bee and its provisions. They pupate in the nest and wait for next spring to emerge as adults.

ORDER	Coleoptera
FAMILY	Meloidae
RANGE	California to Arizona, Northern Sonora, Mexico
SIZE	1/2 to 1 inch

27 · Jerusalem Cricket
Stenopelmatus spp.

ORDER	Orthoptera
FAMILY	Gryllacrididae
RANGE	California to Texas, and most western states from Canada to Mexico
SIZE	1 to 1½ inches

Jerusalem crickets are wingless, long-horned grasshoppers, distant relatives of the more familiar katydids. This bizarre insect may be more than two inches long, with a large, bald head (almost humanoid), and huge, sharp mandibles. The abdomen is brown with black bands, and the legs are adapted for digging. Normally it is found by turning rocks, thus their Spanish name, *niña de la tierra* (child of the earth). Other common names are potato bugs or the Navajo *Wó see ts'inii*, meaning skull insect or bone neck beetle.

Jerusalem crickets are nocturnal predators. They communicate by drumming, striking their body against the substrate to create a specific song now used by scientists to separate the various species found in the western United States. They are related to the famous New Zealand giant land wetas.

An interesting parasite, the horsehair worm, is closely associated with these crickets. Juvenile worms encyst on vegetation the crickets eat. Once inside the cricket, the worm bursts through the gutwall and lives in the body cavity, feeding on, but not harming its host too much. When mature, the worm causes the cricket to move to an aquatic site, then exits its host and enters the water to find a mate and begin a new cycle. The Jerusalem cricket dies nearby.

Robert and Linda Mitchell

28 · Kissing Bug
Triatoma rubida

Allan Morgan

The reduviid family typically consists of assassin bugs, predators of other insects. The triatomes took a different path of evolution and feed on mammalian blood, generally living with ground-nesting animals like packrats and armadillos. With the movement of human populations out of cities and into the rural areas where these mammals reside, triatomes have begun to feed on us, too.

Common names for this blood-feeder are cone-nosed bugs, Hualupai tigers, and kissing bugs. The latter name came from the behavior of feeding near the lips, usually the most exposed skin of a sleeping person.

Kissing bugs feed by piercing the skin and injecting salivary juices that inhibit blood clotting and open capillaries for greater blood flow. The bugs have very fine stylets that do not cause pain or irritation to the host during feeding, reducing the chance that the host will dislodge the bug. The kissing bugs of the Southwest leave the host soon after feeding and defecate in a hidden spot. This fortunate behavior prevents the bug from spreading a pathogen, *Trypanosoma cruzi*, which causes Chagas' disease. The pathogen is found in fecal material and must be rubbed into the wound to cause infection.

Kissing bug adults typically leave host sites in May and June when nighttime temperatures stay above seventy degrees Fahrenheit. They fly away in search of mates. This is when they encounter human residences and may enter. If all events occur properly, including mating and taking a blood meal, the female may lay eggs in the house, which will hatch in late July or August. This starts another population cycle.

ORDER	Hemiptera
FAMILY	Reduviidae
RANGE	California to Texas, Mexico
SIZE	3/4 inch

29 · Leaf-Cutter Bee
Megachile chilopsidis

ORDER	Hymenoptera
FAMILY	Megachilidae
RANGE	Florida to California, north to Colorado, Nebraska, and Kansas
SIZE	1/4 to 1/2 inches

When most people think of bees, they think of honeybees. In the Southwest, bees come in a multitude of designs, colors, and behaviors. The aridity here usually induces ground-nesting behavior, for being underground affords moisture and protection from the weather.

Leaf-cutter bees have evolved a unique method creating cells and protecting their young. These bees seek leaves or flower petals from various plants. Upon locating an appropriate leaf, the bee cuts a perfect circle from the leaf, curls it between its legs, and flies off to some secluded location to start making a cell. The bee may make three or four trips before having enough material to finish a cell. It then provisions the cell with bee bread, a mixture of pollen and nectar gathered from cactus flowers or other supply stations, such as mesquite, acacia, and palo verde. One can recognize the leaf-cutter at work collecting pollen, for it tamps its abdomen on the stamens in the flower, causing pollen to collect on its belly.

With this supply, it returns to the cell, forms the loaf, and finally lays an egg in the cell and closes it. Now the bee can set off for more leaf material and continue building a chain of cells just like the first one.

Allan Morgan

30 · Leaf-Footed Bug
Acanthocephala thomasi

Rick and Nora Bowers

The leaf-footed bugs present many different associations to people. Just sitting on plants, they appear as gangly-legged, spider-like bugs. When they take flight, their noise and movements are almost wasp-like. Their orange-tipped antennae and feet flash in the sunlight.

The common name for this group describes not just the feet but the legs. Males of this species have enlarged femurs and tibiae armed with spines, for this is how males hold the females during courtship and mating. It is not a violent behavior, merely a tactic to ensure effective copulation. Female hind legs are more flattened with almost a leaf-like design, possibly a means of displaying to males when the time is right.

These bugs are common throughout the spring and summer in the Southwest, gathering in groups on the legumes in the canyons and valleys. They have beaks that penetrate the soft plant tissues to drink the nourishing liquids flowing to the plant leaves. If disturbed by some animal, they may take flight, leaving behind a very potent scent to discourage predators.

Although *Acanthocephala thomasi* have long beaks, the only tissues they penetrate are of plants; they don't bite humans.

ORDER	Hemiptera
FAMILY	Coreidae
RANGE	California to Texas
SIZE	1 1/4 inches

31 · Mud Dauber
Sceliphron caementarium

ORDER	Hymenoptera
FAMILY	Sphecidae
RANGE	Most of the Western Hemisphere
SIZE	5/8 to 7/8 inch

Robert and Linda Mitchell

The thread-waisted wasps of the family Sphecidae, so named because of their thin, elongated abdomen, present a very diverse group of predators. Many dig nests in the soil and provision them with grasshoppers, caterpillars, or other juicy insects, sometimes carrying prey twice their size. Many of these soil nesters memorize landmarks to guide them back to the nest site.

The mud dauber, though, has become an expert mason. Taking soil and mixing it with saliva to make a mud composition, she fashions a linear series of columns similar to a pipe organ, hence a common name for this species. Typically you will see these rock-hard nests under bridges, eaves, or other sheltered, moist sites, like rock outcroppings. The nests usually have five to six columns, but occasionally wasps will erect a mansion with twenty-five or more columns.

Once the wasp completes the shelter, she seeks food to stock each column for a single offspring. These wasps hunt spiders, paralyze them, and stack them neatly inside the column. Amazingly, the wasp typically uses the same species of spiders in the nest. Usually a column will contain six to seven spiders, enough for the larval wasp to finish development and spin a cocoon for pupating inside these cozy rock walls.

32 · Oak Gall
Atrusca bella

Rick and Nora Bowers

Insects are classified by many different characteristics, from structure, behavior, feeding, and life history, to residence. Insects may construct homes, such as the paper wasp nest. They may excavate the soil as ants do. Or they may drill into wood like carpenter bees or wood boring beetles. Gall-making insects use chemistry to induce plants to change the style and composition of tissue they produce, and shape it into a totally uncharacteristic site on the plant to house and feed some juvenile insects.

As the juvenile insects feed, they continue to stimulate the plant to produce this novel tissue, which stops growing only when the insects stop feeding and leave as adults. Adults with mandibles, like *Atrusca bella,* chew their way out, leaving a round exit hole in the globular gall. Others might keep an opening in the gall as it forms, or use chemicals to dissolve their pathway to freedom.

The galls provide protection from the environment and most predators and parasites. The outer tissue hardens, especially in the oak galls, making entry very difficult. Although oaks are an especially good resource for gall makers, insects use a wide range of plants. Many groups of insects have gall makers, including certain flies, aphids, and psyllids. You can find galls on leaves, flowers, petioles, stems, and branches. Benign growths to the host plant, they are an extremely important resource to the insect juveniles. Galls do not overwhelm a plant unless that plant has been under stress from other problems, opening itself to overpopulation.

ORDER	Hymenoptera
FAMILY	Cynipidae
RANGE	Arizona to New Mexico
SIZE	Gall diameter 3/4 to 1 inch

33 · Opuntia Bug
Chelinidea vittiger

ORDER	Hemiptera
FAMILY	Coreidae
RANGE	California to Texas
SIZE	1/2 inch

With their tough skin and overwhelming supply of spines, you would think cacti were immune to feeding by herbivores. However, many insects have found ways to overcome these defenses. Insects have a hard exoskeleton that protects them from being impaled on spines. Opuntia bugs have a sharp, sturdy beak for penetrating that tough outer skin of cacti and are small enough to walk below the spines.

The opuntia bug lays eggs near an outcropping of spines and the young emerge en masse in the spring. You probably wouldn't notice them except that the cactus pad starts to become mottled from their feeding. The young puncture the skin, take a drink, and cause a white spot to appear, a new piece of art in nature's display.

The adults appear in the summer months, a little larger and endowed with wings for a quick escape. With a flash of red from the abdomen, the adult speeds away from trouble. Adults also feed on cactus pads and produce white marks. With enough feeding in one site, the cactus may soon have a peephole as the tissues shrink and the tough skin calluses to close the opening.

Art Evans

34 · Orange Skimmer
Libellula saturata

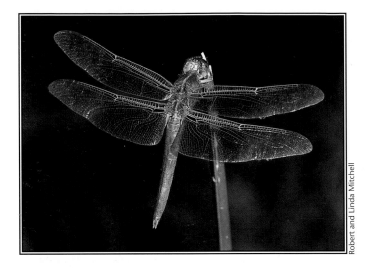

Robert and Linda Mitchell

Dragonflies have always been a delight for people, with their aerobatic feats and pugnacious displays. Dragonflies are without equal in their flight capabilities, zipping along a stream capturing prey in their long legs, turning 180 degrees to escape an entomologist's net, or engaging in dogfights with invaders to their territory. Part of their excellent maneuverability in flight comes from the fact that, unlike other insects, their front and hind wings beat in opposite directions. They are also among the fastest flying insects. The dragonfly head is almost entirely eyes and seems to rotate for 360° vision. No wonder they are great hunters.

Dragonflies are closely tied to aquatic habitats because their juvenile stages, strange predatory nymphs with hinged lower lips for capturing prey, stalk the substrate or plants below water, eating small invertebrates and even fish and tadpoles.

The orange skimmer is the most common species seen here, patrolling pond or stream at about eye level. Sometimes you may see them mating, a strange coupling that looks like a flying heart. When they separate, the male protects the female by hovering above her, while the female flies just above the water, dipping her abdomen into it and releasing eggs.

Their territory may take in fifty square yards, including three or more perches to rest upon. The individual will fly about, alighting, observing, and displaying. Occasionally they may fly out of sight, soon to return to the routine. Notice how different species use different air columns or how competitors try to sneak into foreign territory.

ORDER	Odonata
FAMILY	Libellulidae
RANGE	California to Texas
SIZE	Body 2 inches, Wingspan 3+ inches

35 · Palo Verde Root Borer
Derobrachus geminatus

ORDER	Coleoptera
FAMILY	Cerambycidae
RANGE	California to Texas
SIZE	Adults 3 to 4 inches, Mature larvae up to 5 inches

Summer monsoons in the Southwest signal the beginning of insect activity, a time of aerial displays, music, and drama. This is prime time for mating, and many of the biggest adult insects of the Southwest appear.

The palo verde root borer is a giant brown beetle, well-armed with sharp mandibles and a spiny exoskeleton. It emerges from the soil beneath many different plants in the Southwest, but has been dubbed palo verde root borer for its significant relationship with that tree in Arizona. Farther east in New Mexico, it is called the mesquite root borer.

There are three species in the Southwest and another in the Southeast, but all follow similar patterns. Females burrow into disturbed soil—maybe even their old emergence hole—and lay eggs maybe a foot or so deep near root stock. The eggs hatch and take up to three years to gain proper stature for pupation. They feed on the inner starches of roots. Although on occasion they may cut a root off during feeding, their reputation for killing trees is highly undeserved. They seldom cause problems except for exotic plants that are already under stress from a hostile environment.

Adults are active fliers at dusk, as they seek mates or oviposition sites. Gentle giants until females enter their domain, males may do battle for the right to mate, sometimes biting off part of an antenna or leg.

The larvae have strong mandibles, too. Gas company employees searching for line leaks have found larvae that chewed through the PVC pipe, ending up asphyxiated by their handiwork.

Charles Hedgcock

Larva

Kim Wismann

Adult

36 · Paper Wasp
Polistes flavus

Rick and Nora Bowers

Paper wasps are truly wizards of architecture and manufacturing. The wasps of the Southwest have limited their craft to constructing open, hanging nests, in contrast to their eastern relatives, which build monumental, enclosed structures. These nests are constructed of paper as fine as we use. How can these wasps, with no hands, tools, or manufacturing plants, create this product? They collect available wood fibers, which they chew and mold with their mandibles to create a nest. The caliper sense in the mandibles allows the wasps to produce just the right cell-wall thickness.

Paper wasps are docile until intruders invade the nest territory. The queen and female workers all have stingers (ONLY female wasps, bees, and ants have stingers) and will dive bomb an unsuspecting victim, driving the intruder away in pain. Usually these wasps use their stingers to kill caterpillars and other insects, which they chew up for food, sharing it with the developing larvae in the nest.

Paper wasp queens and males mate in the fall. The males die after mating, but the queens seek shelter to survive the winter. In the early spring, these females emerge, seek good nest sites, and make combs of three to four cells to begin new colonies. The queens lay eggs in the top of these cells and care for these firstborn larvae.

The queen adds additional paper to accommodate the growing larvae. In about two months, the larva caps the cell with a white silky material, signaling pupation. Soon new female wasps appear. The mature wasps build more cells, the queen lays more eggs, and the colony grows throughout the summer.

ORDER	Hymenoptera
FAMILY	Vespidae
RANGE	California to Texas
SIZE	3/4 inch

37 · Pinacate Beetle
Eleodes obscurus sulcipennis

ORDER	Coleoptera
FAMILY	Tenebrionidae
RANGE	California to Texas
SIZE	7/8 to 11/4 inches

Pinacate beetles are the most recognized insects of the Southwest. These odd black beetles amble about during the day searching for food, but when disturbed, stop and elevate their rear end high in the air. Mess with them more and they will produce a pungent odor that drives almost any organism away. Only the grasshopper mouse is persistent enough to overcome the quinone defense of Pinacate beetles.

The melanism (black pigment) of the body acts as sunscreen, preventing ultraviolet rays from burning these beetles to death as they work during the extreme heat of daylight. I wonder if these beetles ever rest, because they also forage during the nighttime.

There are many species of "stink beetles" in the Southwest, from robust, shiny black species, elongate types with the elytra extended into tails, to the species shown here with deep striations in the elytra. Each species has a variation of the odor theme, with *Eleodes obscurus* having the most offensive odor I have encountered.

Pinacate beetles are detritivores, feeding on dead or decaying organic matter, many times near ant nests. Since most ants will attack foreigners at their nest site, *Eleodes* rubs its legs on the stink gland, repulsing ants that approach it. The adults lay eggs in loose organic materials, where the larvae feed and develop.

Defensive posture
(different species)

38· Praying Mantis
Stagmomantis limbata

Should it be called a *praying* mantis because of its posture or a *preying* mantis because of its predatory behavior? Mantises are recognized by their raptorial forelegs, designed for reaching out, grabbing, and impaling victims on those immense spines. An older article refers to mantises as rearhorses, devil's-horses, praying nuns, intelligence bugs, and devil's riding horses.

Mantis females will produce an ootheca, a hardened structure containing their eggs, which they place on a limb to hide it from most danger. These strange egg cases are the bane of schoolteachers, because students bring them into the classroom in the winter, which causes quick development, and one morning the classroom is filled with baby mantises eating each other.

Female mantises typically have shortened wings and a robust abdomen for handling egg production. Males are much thinner with long wings, making them able flyers. In some species, males have a ventral, cyclopean ear tuned in to bat echolocation wavelengths. When alerted to this danger, a male mantis changes flight patterns to escape the bat, becoming an aerobatic ace.

Allan Morgan

ORDER	Mantodea
FAMILY	Mantidae
RANGE	Arizona to Texas, Mexico
SIZE	2 inches

39 · Predatory Ground Beetle
Calosoma peregrinator

Charles Hedgcock

ORDER	Coleoptera
FAMILY	Carabidae
RANGE	California to Texas
SIZE	3/4 to 1 inch

The standard insect description is black, beetle-like with six legs. For once, this fits the creature, for *Calosoma peregrinator* is hard and shiny black. A spectacular variation of this theme is *C. scrutator*, called the fiery searcher because of its metallic green elytra (hardened front wings) lined with purple, and its steely blue legs. Most in this group hunt caterpillars, racing about on the ground with mandibles at the ready. If the ground search is in vain, they may even climb trees to find food.

The juveniles, active elongated larvae, are also predatory and seek similar food as their parents do, wandering the ground or even climbing trees to find soft-bodied insects and caterpillars.

The adults are readily found around artificial lighting systems at night, taking full advantage of the unsuspecting insects that fly to the lights. These beetles do climb, but their true agility is in their cursorial legs, a design that a sprinter would love. Very few prey can outrun one of these beetles.

40 · Rainbow Grasshopper
Dactylotum bicolor

Kim Wismann

A splash of color jumps past as you wander through the grasslands. It's an artistic canvas against the browns and greens of the habitat. As you catch up and stare, a short-winged grasshopper takes shape before you, a totally unexpected animal. In people's perspective, only butterflies should be so magnificent, not a lowly grasshopper. In the Southwest we call it the Mexican general to honor the brilliant uniforms of our neighbors to the south. *Dactylotum*'s colorfulness has earned it other names, like pictured or barber pole grasshopper.

Dactylotum bicolor feeds on desert broom, snakeweed, and burroweed, probably obtaining some of the chemicals that make it so distasteful to predators. That allows these hoppers to then advertise, in essence, their warning: "Don't even think about eating me."

The females lay eggs toward the end of October, a way for this species to survive the winter conditions. The nymphs emerge in the spring, feeding and growing until June, when they molt into adults.

ORDER	Orthoptera
FAMILY	Acrididae
RANGE	Western Texas to Arizona, south into Mexico, in grasslands and desert, usually on gravelly soils
SIZE	Males 7/8 inch, Females 1 1/4 inches

ORDER	Diptera
FAMILY	Asilidae
RANGE	Widespread in the United States
SIZE	1/4 to 1 inch or more depending on species

Flies are a very downtrodden group of insects, mostly thought of as garbage feeders or fruit destroyers. When a group of flies suddenly shows up as aggressive predators, one has to take notice. That is the family Asilidae. These flies, equipped with a very sharp beak hidden behind a beard, will attack even wasps and bees to gain a dinner.

Efferia and many closely related genera are usually gray with some white markings, nothing to cause notice until you see their speed of attack. Some bedeck themselves in bumblebee mimicry, the bright yellow and black hairs protecting them from other predators as they perch in the flowers. There are even species that mimic tarantula wasps, those grand black and orange spider hunters. All seek insects for prey.

Even if their colors are bland, their behavior catches the eye. First a quick flight to a perch, a survey of the territory, and then off to the next perch, flying close to the ground.

The larvae of robber flies live in the soil and seek other insects to eat. As you might expect, following larvae as they burrow through the soil is not an easy task, so researchers know little about the prey or how long *Efferia* spends as a juvenile.

Rick and Nora Bowers

42 · Seed Bug
Lygaeus kalmii

Cecil Schwalbe

When people take the time to look down and see the small, they realize how omnipresent insects are. You may not have noticed seed bugs, but they are a dominant insect in our landscape.

This species has dynamic coloration: red, gray, and black with two white spots near the end of its wings. People sometimes mistake it for the box elder bug, a species well known because of the abundance of box elder trees used in landscaped settings.

Lygaeus kalmii is common because it seeks out the wide variety of seeds scattered on the ground. Its population skyrockets in years when plant production is good. The ground becomes a living carpet of bugs scurrying about in search of food. Although some people view them as a nuisance, seed bugs manage plant populations by preventing excessive seed germination.

ORDER	Hemiptera
FAMILY	Lygaeidae
RANGE	Western United States
SIZE	3/8 inch

43 · Shore Earwig
Labidura riparia

ORDER	Dermaptera
FAMILY	Labiduridae
RANGE	Arizona to Texas
SIZE	3/4 to 1 inch

Robert and Linda Mitchell

Robert and Linda Mitchell

Earwigs are familiar but misunderstood insects because of the common name and the menacing pincers at the rear guard. Early Anglo-Saxons called them *earwicga* (eare = ear and wicga = beetle or worm). These people lived in sod huts and slept on straw mattresses, good habitat for the insects, which would then walk into the ears of sleepers while hunting for food at night. Unfortunately, horror television shows created the myth about earwigs penetrating one's brain and laying eggs there, with the young eventually eating the brain. The pincers, although strong enough to capture insects, cannot hurt people.

The shore earwig is the largest of southwestern species, with the male pincers (forceps) extremely robust. They have shortened forewings and fanlike hindwings. This species is well known in agricultural fields, burrowing under stones or debris into moist soil, hunting at night for caterpillars or other soft-bodied insects and earthworms. Although some earwigs may take bites from leaves, overall they are a positive component of gardening.

Females protect the eggs and early stages of young, driving away predators with the forceps, an unusual behavior for insects. The nursery area is found in side tunnels, the main tunnels providing mating areas. This species also produces a strong, rancid odor to keep predators away from the nest site.

44 · Spittle Bug
Clastoptera arizonana

Bill Johnson

You rarely see spittle bugs, but you probably notice their work: a white foamy mass termed cuckoo spit. It means the juvenile stage has taken up residence on a blade of grass or succulent twig and begun to feed. These naked nymphs are susceptible to the extreme weather conditions of spring and summer and must devise some protection to survive. The nymphs have special glands on the abdomen that produce a mucilaginous substance that combines with fluids voided from the anus. A specially designed abdominal region equipped with spiracles (breathing pores) bubbles air into this foam, which flows over the insect. This shelter from the weather probably also protects *Clastoptera arizonana* from predators and parasites and allows the nymph to feed and grow in safety.

The adults emerge from the spittle, then fly or jump to other parts of the plant for mating and oviposition into plant stems. The eggs overwinter and emerge when the plant becomes active once more.

ORDER	Hemiptera
FAMILY	Clastopteridae
RANGE	Arizona
SIZE	1/8 inch

45 · Tarantula Hawk
Pepsis thisbe

ORDER	Hymenoptera
FAMILY	Pompilidae
RANGE	California to Texas
SIZE	Body 3/4 to 1 3/4 inches, Wingspan 1 1/4 to 3 inches

A Disney film, *The Living Desert*, certainly gave tarantula hawks a spectacular scene to excite the bugwatchers. The drama of a giant wasp encountering another giant of the Southwest, a tarantula, followed by a battle to the death, seemed almost *Star Wars* in quality. The potential for seeing this event live is very real.

These giant blue-black wasps with brilliant orange wings cruise four to ten feet in the air, occasionally landing and frenetically searching the ground for their prey, the tarantula. If the female wasp encounters a tarantula burrow, she tries to lure the spider out of its lair with subtle touches to the silken door. The two wage a battle for supremacy, usually with the wasp emerging victorious. The wasp must then drag the paralyzed spider back to her burrow, which may take hours. Once home, she places the spider in the burrow and lays one egg on it. The larva hatches in three to four days and attaches to the spider abdomen with its sharp mandibles. It feeds on liquids from the tarantula for its first four growth stages. In its fifth stage, the larva chews into the tarantula and consumes much of the innards, killing the spider. The larva, now more than two inches long, spins a cocoon and pupates inside. This drama underground requires 250 to 350 days, when the new wasp finally digs out from the burrow.

Males establish territories on hillsides with flowering trees as a lure for females. Females fly past these territories, select a lucky male, and mate. Often throughout the summer, flowering trees are abuzz with these wasps feeding. Do not become alarmed at their presence, for they have a directed activity to keep them busy. The only aggression they may show is toward a tarantula.

Tarantula hawk attacking a tarantula

Robert and Linda Mitchell

46· Ten-Striped June Beetle
Polyphylla decimlineata

Art Evans

The ten-striped June beetle, named for the ten white stripes on the elytra and its appearance during the month of June, feeds late at night (9:30 to 11). Specific activity periods like this are common for many insects. Timing is everything, whether for feeding, mating, or avoiding predators.

The larval stage lives in sandy soil, where it feeds on roots of such plants as coniferous seedlings, strawberries, blueberries, and mint. After a summer of feeding the larvae burrow about three feet deep for the winter. It takes about three to four years for the larvae to mature as they move between roots and warm harborage. They emerge as adults in summer and feed on needles of ponderosa pine, Norway spruce, and Douglas fir.

The adults are quite noisy when disturbed, making squeaking noises by rubbing the pygidium (a plate on the posterior of the abdomen) and the elytra together, a process called stridulation. They may make noise to startle predators, causing them to leave these potential dinner morsels alone.

ORDER	Coleoptera
FAMILY	Scarabaeidae
RANGE	Western United States, Southwestern Canada, and Northern Mexico
SIZE	1 inch

ORDER	Coleoptera
FAMILY	Carabidae
RANGE	California to Texas and Baja California
SIZE	1/4 inch

Tiger beetles catch the eye because most are metallic green, blue, red, or bronze. They are the roadrunners of the bug world, sprinting across the landscape in search of other insects to eat. They can fly also, which aids them when they need to escape.

Tiger beetle larvae live in holes with their head held at an angle to the surface, waiting for unsuspecting insects to walk past. The larva pops out of the hole and snatches the bug with its huge sickle-shaped mandibles, pulling it into the hole where it drinks the juices of its prey.

The adult has huge chewing mandibles held in front of the head, so as it runs, its capturing device is always at the ready. Colors of adults are quite complex. In an internal layer of the exoskeleton, melanin is formed in a series of thin sublayers, which reflect and absorb different colors. The outer exoskeleton is embossed with raised granules and small depressions, each causing different reflections resulting in metallic coloration. Although it would seem that such brilliant colors would give away these beetles, in reality they create a cryptic effect and hide the beetles from predators.

Even more startling has been the discovery of a pair of tympanic hearing organs located on the abdomen but hidden from sight by the elytra. These tympana respond to ultrasound. *C. lemniscata* is active both day and night, and the "ears" help them elude echolocating bats. Most other tiger beetles are only day-active, but a primary predator, the robber fly, produces ultrasound wingbeat frequencies that would be detectable by the beetle ears.

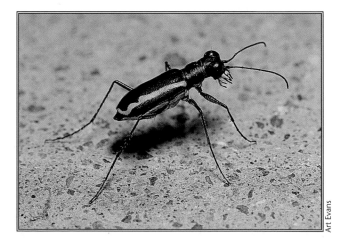

Art Evans

48· Velvet Ant
Dasymutilla magnifica

Marty Cordano

Velvet ants have a secret: They are really wasps. The female is wingless and appears very antlike, with long hairs covering her body, hence the name.

In the Southwest, this group is very diverse, but *Dasymutilla magnifica* is the most striking. Mutillids are diurnal (day-active) or nocturnal (night-active). Diurnal species are spectacularly colored (reds, yellows, and blacks) to advertise their protection, a potent sting that should make the stingee more wary of the next encounter. Entomologists call this aposematic coloration. In all Hymenoptera, it is the female that possesses the stinger, a modified ovipositor (egg-laying device). The sting is used most often for paralyzing prey, food for adults and offspring, but is also an effective defense against predators.

Mutillids use ground-nesting bees, wasps, and several other groups of insects as food for their offspring. The females will enter a nest when the host larva has already pupated, lay one or two eggs on the pupa, and leave the nest. Because they have no wings, females successfully dig through soil without risk of damaging delicate wing structures. The eggs hatch, devour the host pupa, and pupate themselves. Depending on the species, they may have one or two generations a year. The host for *D. magnifica* is not known.

The name cow-killer has long been part of the folklore of mutillids. The sting is quite powerful, and stories abound of a cow grazing and accidentally getting one of these wasps into its mouth and having it sting the tongue, which then swells and suffocates the animal. We may think cows are stupid, but this seems far-fetched.

ORDER	Hymenoptera
FAMILY	Mutillidae
RANGE	California to Texas
SIZE	7/8 inch

49 · Webspinner
Oligotoma nigra

ORDER	Embiidina
FAMILY	Oligotomidae
RANGE	Arizona to Texas
SIZE	1/4 inch

Webspinners are a small, unique order of insects, mostly tropical but represented in the Southwest by several introduced species. They are an oddity because their front feet ("tarsi" in bug lingo) are modified with spinning glands, appearing clublike.

You may find the silken tubes that webspinners call home under rocks or debris. Females are wingless, never leaving their tubes but attracting the males with sexual pheromones (odors). They feed on organic debris, which they may incorporate into their silken tubes.

The males are the ones readily seen by people in the Southwest because they are good fliers and come into homes, attracted by light at night. They are small, maybe a quarter-inch or more in length, brown in color, and hold their wings flat over the body. They seem to be a curious lot, for when you stare at a webspinner, it can cock its head and peer back at you. Because of their small stature, they easily come through your screens and hang out on your book or computer screen.

Think of these visitors as a rare treat, for entomologists come from all over the country just to find this order of insects. They are harmless, simply seeking friendship after being drawn from their natural habitat by your bright lights.

50 · White-Lined Sphinx Moth
Hyles lineata

Rick and Nora Bowers

Allan Morgan

The caterpillar stage of the sphinx moth makes its presence known, sometimes overwhelmingly, while the adult is noticed less often because it is nocturnal. We notice the adult white-lined sphinx moth for its ability to hover near flowers while extending its elongate proboscis to drink from the nectaries. Many people think they are watching hummingbirds until they look more closely. The moth feeds during the day, but is also active at night-blooming flowers. Because of their large population, these moths are some of the most important pollinators in the Southwest.

After the summer rains begin, the yellowish-green caterpillar stage of the sphinx moth starts its massive march to new territory, searching for soil easy to burrow into. During this time, the two-to-three-inch-long caterpillar dominates the landscape, with possibly millions of individuals creeping along. They may eat a bit on plants, but mostly they seek a pupation spot. Although the species has several generations during the year only the last batch stages a fall parade.

The Tohono O'odham used to take advantage of this windfall of animals, harvesting, prepping, and drying them to provide a fantastic source of high-protein, low-fat, low-cholesterol food for the winter.

ORDER	Lepidoptera
FAMILY	Sphingidae
RANGE	Throughout the United States
SIZE	Caterpillar 2 to 3 inches, Adult wingspan 2 1/2 inches

GLOSSARY

Alates winged reproductive forms of termites, ants, and aphids

Aposematic bright coloring—such as orange and black, red and black, yellow and black—that advertises having bad taste or other defensive features and warns away predators

Arthropod term used to classify closely related animals, including trilobites (extinct), crustaceans (lobsters, crabs, shrimp), spiders, scorpions, mites, centipedes, millipedes, and insects

Cryptic, Crypsis colors and shapes of animals that help them blend into their background

Elytra the hardened front wings of beetles

Genus (plural genera) taxonomic term used to describe closely related animals, the first word, always capitalized, in a species name. For example, *Scotoleon niger: Scotoleon* is the genus antlion, *niger* the species designation of a particular species of antlion.

Habitat the natural area where an animal resides

Larva (plural larvae) immature stage of insects that undergo complete metamorphosis; maggot, grub, and caterpillar are group-specific names for larvae

Mandibles the chewing mouthparts of insects

Malpighian tubes waste-removal organs found in the abdomen

Ovipositor egg-laying structure, modified in wasps, bees, and ants as a stinging device

Petiole the thin waist of a wasp

Pheromones chemicals emitted as communication between individuals of the same species resulting in some behavioral response, like mating or defense

Pronotum the top hardened first segment of the thorax (middle body region of insects); in grasshoppers this appears like a saddle behind the head

Pygidium the hardened last segment of the abdomen (third body region of insects)

Reduviid a common name derived from a family of insects called assassin bugs, kissing bugs

Stridulation communicative sounds created by insects, made by rubbing two modified body parts together, like rubbing a pencil across a comb. The modified structures are termed files and scrapers.

FURTHER READING

Alcock, J., and T. Forsyth (illustrator). *In a Desert Garden: Love and Death Among the Insects*, Tucson, Ariz.: University of Arizona Press, 1999.

Alcock, J., and M. H. Stewart (illustrator). *Sonoran Desert Spring*. Tucson, Ariz.: University of Arizona Press, 1994.

Alcock, J., and M. H. Stewart (illustrator). *Sonoran Desert Summer*. Tucson, Ariz.: University of Arizona Press, 1994.

Bailowitz, R., and D. Danforth. *70 Common Butterflies of the Southwest*. Tucson, Ariz.: Western National Parks Association, 1997.

Stewart, B. *Common Butterflies of California*. Arcata, Calif.: West Coast Lady Press, 1997.

Stewart, B., P. Brodkin, and H. Brodkin. *Butterflies of Arizona: A Photographic Guide*. Arcata, Calif.: West Coast Lady Press, 2001.

Werner, F., and C. Olson. *Insects of the Southwest*. Tucson, Ariz.: Fisher Books, 1994.

INDEX

Acanthocephala thomasi, 30

Anax junius, 20

Angle-winged katydid, 19

Ant, harvester, 22

Ant, velvet, 48

Antlion, 1

Apiomerus flaviventris, 3

Apis mellifera, 23

Arenivaga erratica, 12

Ascalapha odoratus, 4

Atrusca bella, 32

Bagworm, 2

Bee
"Africanized," 23
carpenter, 5
honeybee, 23
"killer," 23
leafcutter, 29

Bee killer, 3

Black witch, 4

Blister beetle, iron-cross, 26

Calosoma peregrinator, 39

Canthon imitator, 14

Carpenter bee, 5

Chelinidea vittiger, 33

Cholla long-horned beetle, 6

Chrysoperla carnea, 21

Cicada, 7

Cicindela lemniscata, 47

Clastoptera arizonana, 44

Cochineal scales, 8

Cockroach, sand, 12

Cone-nosed bug, 28

Convergent ladybird beetle, 9

Cotinus mutabilis, 15

Crane fly, 10

Creosote walkingstick, 11

Cricket, Jerusalem, 27

Dactylopius confusus, 8

Dactylotum bicolor, 40

Darner, green, 20

Dasymutilla magnifica, 48

Dauber, mud, 31

Derobrachus geminatus, 35

Desert cockroach, 12

Desert encruster termite, 13

Diapheromera covilleae, 11

Diceroprocta semicincta, 7

Dung beetle, 14

Earwig, shore, 43

Efferia spp., 41

Eleodes obscurus sulcipennis, 37

Encruster termite, 13

Fig beetle, 15

Firefly, 16

Fly
hover, 25
robber, 41

Gall, oak, 32

Giant mesquite bug, 17

Gnathamitermes perplexus, 13

Grasshopper, rainbow, 40

Gray bird locust, 18

Greater angle-winged katydid, 19

Green darner, 20

Green lacewing, 21

Ground beetle, predatory, 39

Harvester ant, 22

Hippodamia convergens, 9

Honeybee, 23

Horse lubber, 24

Hover fly, 25

Hualupai tiger, 28

Hyles lineata, 50

Iron-cross blister beetle, 26

Jerusalem cricket, 27

June beetle, 15, 46

Katydid, angle-winged, 19

Kissing bug, 28

Labidura riparia, 43

Lacewing, green, 21

Lady bug, 9

Ladybird beetle, 9

Leaf-cutter bees, 29

Leaf-footed bug, 30

Libellula saturata, 34

Lightningbug, 16

Locust, 18

Long-horned beetle, 6

Lubber, horse, 24

Lygaeus kalmii, 42

Mantis, praying, 38

Megachile chilopsidis, 29

Mesquite bug, 17

Microcentrum rhombifolium, 19

Moneilema gigas, 6

Moth, white-lined sphinx, 50

Mud dauber, 31

Oak gall, 32

Oiketicus toumeyi, 2

Oligotoma nigra, 49

Opuntia bug, 33

Orange skimmer, 34

Palo verde root borer, 35

Paper wasp, 36

Pepsis thisbe, 45

Pinacate beetle, 37
Pleotomus nigripennis, 16
Pogonomyrmex rugosus, 22
Polistes flavus, 36
Polyphylla decimlineata,
    46
Praying mantis, 38
Predatory ground beetle,
    39

Rainbow grasshopper, 40
Robber fly, 41
Root borer, palo verde, 35

Sceliphron caementarium,
    31
Schistocerca nitens, 18
Scotoleon niger, 1

Seed bug, 42
Shore earwig, 43
Skimer, orange, 34
Sphinx moth, white-lined,
    50
Spittle bug, 44
Stagmomantis limbata, 38
Stenopelmatus spp., 27
Stink bug, 37

Taeniopoda eques, 24
Tarantula hawk, 45
Tegrodera aloga, 26
Ten-striped June beetle,
    46
Termite, desert encruster,
    13
Thasus neocalifornicus, 17

Tiger beetle, 47
Tipula spp., 10
Triatoma rubida, 28

Velvet ant, 48
Volucella isabellina, 25

Walkingstick, creosote, 11
Wasp
    Mud dauber, 31
    paper, 36
Webspinner, 49
White-lined sphinx moth,
    50

*Xylocopa californica
    arizonensis,* 5

ABOUT THE AUTHOR

Carl A. Olson, Associate Curator of the Department of Entomology at the University of Arizona, has followed insects large and small, exotic and common, since he first noticed their busy lives. He has a special interest in the way humans have related to insects throughout their mutual history.